Somebody Stole My Smile!

by Carmen Tafolla

illustrated by Tammie Lyon

ISBN: 0-328-17010-0

Copyright © Pearson Education, Inc.
All Rights Reserved. Printed in the United States of America. This publication is protected by Copyright, and permission should be obtained from the publisher prior to any prohibited reproduction, storage in a retrieval system, or transmission in any form by any means, electronic, mechanical, photocopying, recording, or otherwise. For information regarding permission(s), write to: Permissions Department, Scott Foresman, 1900 East Lake Avenue, Glenview, Illinois 60025.

3 4 5 6 7 8 9 10 V008 12 11 10 09 08 07

When I was six, I had very long brown hair, straight white teeth, and green eyes.

My family lived in a tiny blue-and-white house in an old Mexican neighborhood. Our backyard had a swing and a big, shady peach tree.

Every day I played outside with our old cat in the hot Texas summer. It was quiet and peaceful. And nothing changed.

Each morning, I looked in the mirror and saw a face and a smile I liked.

Everyone in my family had brown eyes except me. But the old cat had green eyes too. So I smiled and felt okay.

One day I looked in the mirror and my smile was gone. The new smile had a big hole in the middle!

Oh, I remember! Last night during supper I lost a tooth as I bit into a hot, buttery tortilla.

My tooth dropped out.
My mother said, "Now you're growing up." But I didn't understand. I had NOT looked into the mirror.

Today I saw a girl in the mirror with hair and eyes like mine, but SHE had a smile with a hole in the middle!

"Mama!" I cried. "Do I look funny?"
"No, of course not, *mijita*," she said.
My sister pointed at me and giggled.

The face that I used to see in the mirror wasn't there anymore. Where did my old smile go?

I went out to my swing in the backyard. But the backyard looked odd too! The pink flowers on the peach tree were missing.

"Mama! The peach tree lost its flowers!"
"Good, *mijita*, that means peaches will begin to grow."

I was upset. I did not like my new smile. I did not like the tree with no flowers. I did not like these changes!

As summer passed,
I hopped on the
sidewalk squares and
played on the swing.

I petted the old cat and ate hot, buttery tortillas.

Every day I would look in the mirror. There was still an empty spot in my smile.

One day, while petting the cat, I felt something hit me on the head. Thump! It was a juicy, ripe peach!

I ran inside yelling, "Mama! You were right! New peaches are growing from the tree!"

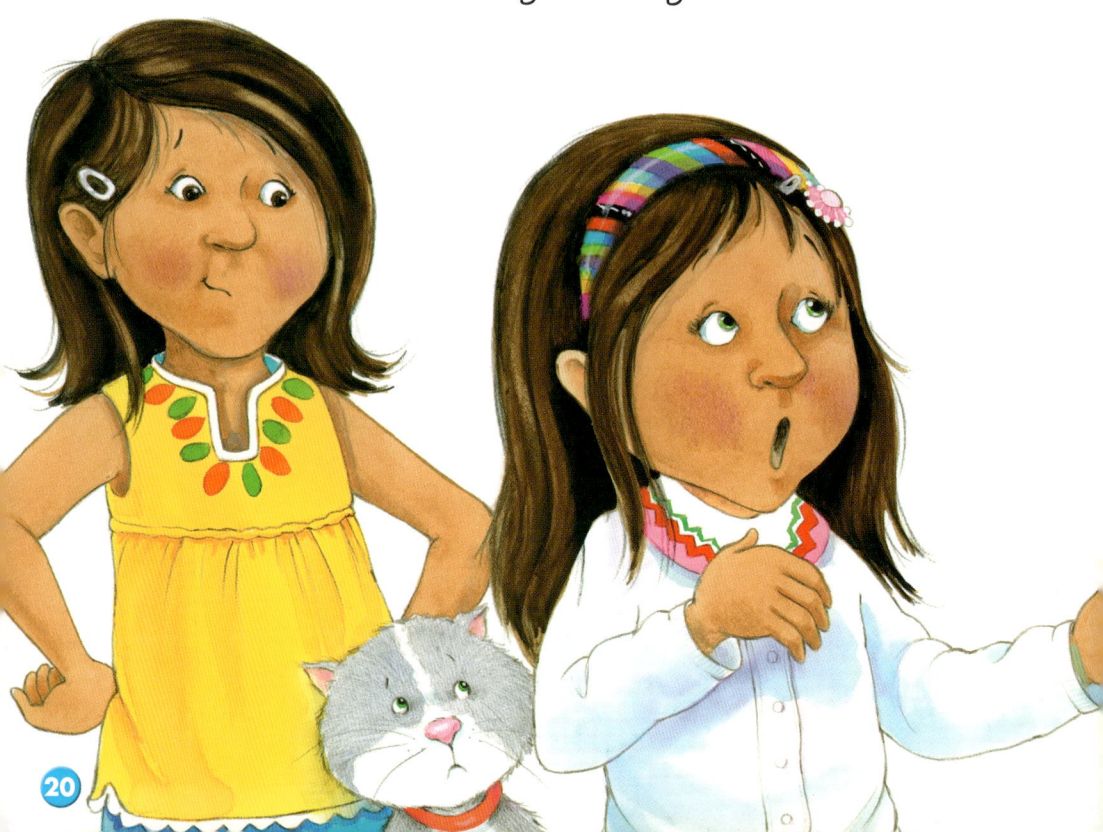

"That's not the only new thing that's growing," she said.

I looked into the mirror. There, instead of the odd hole in my smile, was the tip of a new tooth, a growing-up tooth. And I liked it!

I said to my mother, "Some changes are kind of nice." Then I counted all the new peaches growing where flowers had been.

Epilogue by Carmen Tafolla:
Today I am a grown woman, and my children are growing up too. My children long ago lost all their baby teeth and have grown their adult teeth. But my sister, who is old, has lost several of her teeth. That's okay. Life changes. Today, she loves what she calls my green "cat eyes." I love her beautiful almond brown eyes. And we both think that a smile is the most beautiful thing of all, no matter what teeth are there!

Glossary:
Mijita is the short version of *mi hijita*, which means "my daughter" in Spanish. Many Mexican American parents call their children (and all children they like) *mijita* (my daughter) and *mijito* (my son) as a way of saying they care.